This book is dedicated to Little Lottie, and all the children that will grow up to be their ancestors' wildest dreams.

You 're beautiful, smart and powerful. Continue learning and never stop dreaming!

A is for API

An API is the contact point like where puzzle pieces meet.
When connected they make something really sweet.

B

is for   **Blockchain**

Blockchain is like a long receipt,
All transactions are forever
kept nice and neat.

C

is for

Code

Code is the building blocks that make software run.
That's what makes
learning to code so much fun.

```
int num;
    printf("Enter an integer:
        scanf("%d", &num);

#include <std
int main() {
    int n, i;
    printf("Enter an i
    scanf("%d", &n);
    for (i = 1; i <= 10; ++i
        printf("%d * %d =
}
    return 0;
}

sum = number1 + number2;

#include <stdio.h>
int main() {

    (num % 2 == 0) ? printf("%d is ev
    printf("%d is odd,",num);
        return 0;

const originalString
```

D
is for
Database

Information can be stored in a
Database. To organize data
this is the best place.

is for **Engineer**

An Engineer is a special technician.
Building software and hardware, that is her mission.

F is for Firewall

To protect your computer, build a Firewall.
It's a security guard that you can't see at all.

G is for GIF

Your pic will be real jazzy if,
You add an animated GIF.

H is for Hardware

The parts of a computer are called Hardware.
Open it up to see what is in there.

I is for iPhone

There was one more thing to make the phone even better. Now you can touch a screen for each letter.

J is for JavaScript

JavaScript can be used to build a website.
It sure is one clever code tool all right.

K is for Keyboard

A Keyboard has letters and numbers on keys.
It's how you enter things on your Mac or PC.

is for **Link**

W W W.

W W W.

With a Link you can go to webpages real fast.
You can move through the internet quickly at last.

M is for Malware

**Malware is like a virus that infects your PC,
And causes real damage that you cannot see.**

N is for Network

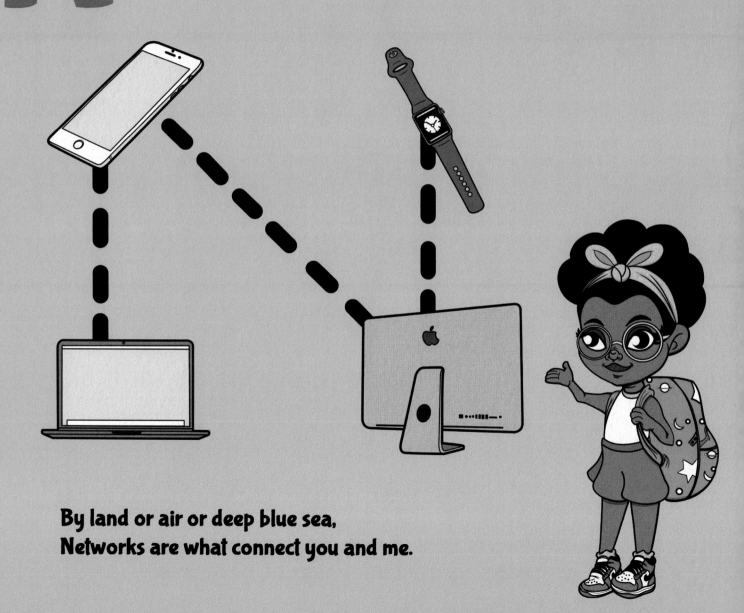

By land or air or deep blue sea,
Networks are what connect you and me.

 **is for Open Source**

Share your coding with all with Open Source.
Everyone agrees that it's great, of course.

P

is for **Python**

Python is used to create special functions.
The best way to perform a set of instructions.

Q is for Query

A Query lets you ask a computer a question.
Saying, "Hey Siri!" is just one suggestion.

R is for Reboot

**If your computer gets out of whack,
Just do a Reboot to bring it right back.**

 **is for** **Software**

**Software on your computer, phone or TV,
tells these things just what to do, you see.**

T is for Terminal

Hello.

The Terminal was the very first,
Digital computer in the universe.

U is for **User Interface**

To work with a computer in any place,
You do it through a User Interface.

V is for Virtual Reality

A VR computer can make you feel,
Like you're in a world that is very real.

W is for Wifi

**WiFi networks send data through the air.
No need for wires or other hardware.**

X

is for

XLS

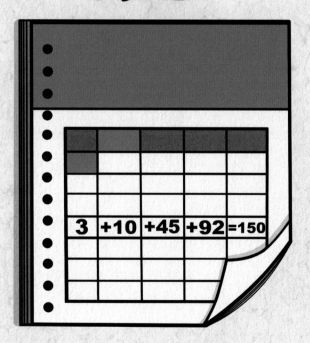

3	+10	+45	+92	=150

There is a file called an XLS.
This file calculates numbers the best.

Y

is for

YouTube

YouTube lets people share videos.
It's a good place to learn, everyone knows.

Z is for **Zip Drive**

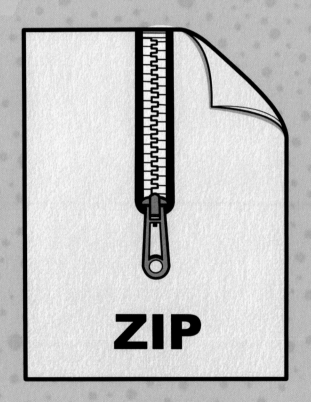

ZIP

You're done with this book, give yourself a high five, and save this book in your own Zip Drive.

Made in the USA
Las Vegas, NV
26 October 2020